POEMS

IAIN BANKS

AND

KEN MACLEOD

POEMS

IAIN BANKS

AND

KEN MACLEOD

Little, Brown

LITTLE, BROWN

First published in Great Britain in 2015 by Little, Brown

1 3 5 7 9 10 8 6 4 2

A CIP catalogue record for this book
is available from the British Library.

ISBN 978-1-4087-0587-2

Typeset in Sabon by Palimpsest Book Production Ltd,
Falkirk, Stirlingshire
Printed and bound in Great Britain by Clays Ltd, St Ives plc

Papers used by Little, Brown are from well-managed
forests and other responsible sources.

MIX
Paper from
responsible sources
FSC® C104740

Little, Brown
An imprint of
Little, Brown Book Group
100 Victoria Embankment
London EC4Y 0DY

An Hachette UK Company
www.hachette.co.uk

www.littlebrown.co.uk

CONTENTS

Poems by Ken MacLeod

Introduction: Songs of Stone

Iain Banks the literary novelist and Iain M. Banks the science-fiction writer are too well known to need introduction, but Iain Banks the poet has hitherto been almost undetected. A single poem, '041', published in a poetry magazine; two poems ('"Slight Mechanical Destruction"' and 'Zakalwe's Song') book-ending *Use of Weapons*; some lines from 'Feu de Joie' (which he excluded from this collection) embedded in *The Crow Road* (and with much more of its content saturating *A Song of Stone*) have been his only publications. But he took his poetry seriously and worked on it carefully, though he shared the results (about which he had no false modesty) mainly with friends.

As can be seen from the dates, Iain started writing poetry almost as soon as he arrived in high school, and continued until 1981. Why he stopped I can only speculate. The manuscript – handwritten, contents-listed, page-numbered – of the collection, characteristically titled *poems where the heart is*, from which he selected (and sometimes slightly but significantly revised) the poems here, has something of a sense of completion.

Readers of Banks's prose will find in these poems many aspects of his writing with which they're already familiar: a humane and materialist sensibility, an unflinching stare at the damage people can do to each other, a warm appreciation of the joy they can give to each other, a revel in language, a geologically informed gaze on land and sea, a continued meditation on what it means for us to be mortal embodied minds with a fleeting but consequent existence between abysses of deep time.

I too started writing poems in high school, and I've continued to write them, on and off, since. Only 'Faith as a Grain of Poppy Seed' has been published in a poetry magazine; others have appeared in publications of various science-fiction communities and conventions, and one, 'Erosion', was included in the text of my novel *Intrusion*.

Some time in 2012, well before he had any inkling of his illness, Iain said to me that he wanted to see his poems and mine published, preferably together. I demurred; he insisted, and I agreed. He had the risible notion that my poems would provide his with some kind of covering fire. I think the truth is quite the reverse, but in defence of my works' inclusion I can say that – because over the years we read and discussed each other's poems – there is an element of dialogue and evidence of mutual influence.

He continued to work on this project during his illness. A few final revisions to a handful of poems were only found after Iain's death, and I've incorporated them here. For finding the final corrections and the original manuscripts, and for much else, I thank Adele.

Ken MacLeod,
2014

Iain Banks
Poems

Damage

The rags burn, a small pile on the dirty slope of
  beach
Ignored behind the buildings. Waves
Jerk them, sizzling.
Floating sinking, floating sinking
Out.

I

Bless the wind of no direction, that charms the
  flesh
From the blackened bone, that teases the leaf
From the ravaged tree, that demands the
Child from the mother's lap, that parts the two
  then
Parts the one then parts the parts as if it were
Dissatisfied.
    Or on spat pavements, sticky gutters, fouled
      streets
Find your god. Who watches where the rust snakes
Climb the green-stained stones to fasten and suck.
Cracked.
Yellow.
The hand that . . .
    Or the girl perhaps, walking like an interruption
To the morning's chill mundanity, passing the
  beggar
Selling matches on the road to the station

And remembering . . . a sourness from the vine, swallowed
In the dark. The rat,
Twitching on the boards,
Frothing red round its lips.
. . . The snow melts beneath her feet.
    'This is an old house, but—'
This is an old house, and being shown round
Try not to see the boards dead feet have scraped,
Or the crumbling enamel under stained windows
Pinioned under the sun, peering at the stagnant sand,
Wallowing in the sight of the sea,
Steeped, in the child's tears, burning.   There were.
'There were even bullet holes in the wall. From the war.'
    And the hand that.
Bless death, that crime, which is its own punishment,
And on the battlefield let there be war,
For as the pearl is the daughter of the oyster's torment,
As the mink must die to save its skin
And as the infant enters, disengaging, through a maw of pain,
So must death be . . . cajoled, to play a proper part.
    Before he leaves, he cuts the stray dark lock,
Then lays down the scissors, lifts the map, and with the
Keys, and having checked everything, leaves.
– He remembers night, sleep, the bed, their shared comas,

A certain source of fondness in the night.
(She saw, no, expected, a dawn from every light.
Such was her fault)
And the hand that cupped the breast, strikes the
    child.

II

In the basement, the fire burns, a contained
    combustion,
Fury in iron, clothed in rust, self-consuming mixer.
Sweet fire sour fire, flames not tongues nor hands
    nor face
But flames alone.
They accepted what she gave, insinuating within
    the bundle
Of sheets an undemanding rage,
Expiating
A white, committed sin.
While the walls did not echo to the things she did
    not say.
    Mme Mercure is on the train now, worming its
        way
By predetermined ways, flowing from snow to
    slush, land cold
Under a low sun. She reads a magazine.
She has a plastic cup of coffee, and,
Annoyed by a recalcitrant lash,
Plucks out the blonde offender
With tweezers.
Once she saw his thumb turn down, then turning
    up, pressed
Forward, and against the window, crushed a fly.

The man that . . .
    So are the dead heaped in piles of one,
Spattered like the bull's blood spattered, falling
Under the broken sun, broken as the chicken's
    neck, jerked
Powerless as the child under the tank;
Just a hunk of meat with a brain, with time to
    choose
To laugh once
Or cry once
But not both.
– See us seduced by fire and water,
And sweet *Enola*'s kiss.

        The bird flies, glittering blue in an azure sky.
        The bird flies, for ever, over the drowned planet.
        The bird flies, blue feathers over endless cobalt
            waves.
        And gives no clue on which blue sign
        There rests the hint, the accusation
        Of the fire that burns,
        At the core.

Ferris at the level crossing, stopped in the middle
Of a long journey, watching pale streaks of faces
Flame briefly in the gloom of the passing train,
Puts on gloves.
It is growing colder, slush on roads,
And he has learned too-cold metal burns just as
    well.
He recalls that she demanded 'Why am I?'
        And would not take her echo as an answer.
. . . He feels . . . like an old pop star,

Tossing and turning in the darkness of a cheap
    hotel,
Kept awake by his past hit, played too loudly in
    the room above.
A man who did not believe in death.
        The ground floor, where he drew the curtains,
Vertical sea staring on to horizontal,
Where, face deepened by the light, he bent to snuff
    the old lamps.
And the old brass bed they bought together;
There were marks on the wall. From hauling it
    upstairs.
The kitchen has a *vast* ancient coal range. Kept on
For show.
Once, when a pan with oil in it went up in flames,
She had to stop him; he wanted to put water on
    it.
        Life or death, scissors and forceps,
Gleaming in the front-street light,
A double operation . . . or conciseness in a scrape.
(She marked it in her English diary.
'Tue' said the day, abbreviated.)
Death. Rhetorical answer to the preceding
    question,
Relying only on itself, depending only on itself.
Or perhaps not so,
Perhaps the stone knows better,
And all that dies was born to live.
Here lies, says the stone, a man who did not
    believe in death.

Esther Mercure, gathering up her things as the
    train slows,
Gazes for a moment at a small piece of skin,
    coming
Away from the flesh at the side of her thumb-nail,
And feels her body, fraying at the edges.
'There was no child. There was never any child.'
– She stands before the house, remembering
    glittering symbols.

    The dead man cries: Dancing, dancing, see us
    dancing
    Sing a song and set us dancing
    Turn your head and leave us kissing
    What the birds of prey refused
    Sell the Sarajevo ticket darling
    Catch a bullet, what's the use? ('follow me, follow
    me')

    And if you have to ask . . .
Ah, the bedroom; scene of, cause of, stage.
Where she cried alone, used cans of spray
Burning walls and windows, furniture and
    floor
Black with dripping paint.
And heaved the bed out crashing down the stairs,
While the room behind her echoed
To the sounds of ancient screams,
Like wax burning, dripping, burning.

Finale. Whose climax the end of life; death's own,
Or life's? *Petit mal, petite mort,* shall we repeat,
'Ah but my dear,
There are at least four ways to explain
  everything'?
Or stick to the unchallengeable, such as
'Cars die young' and 'no change out of a missile'?
Such individualism; not so much a philosophy,
More of an excuse.
And if you have to ask, if you have to *ask.*

See. Andrew Ferris, striding angrily from the bell
Unanswering. A wasted journey,
Lying bleeding on the stones
There was no child. There was never any child.
And on the way to the station car park
Snatches at the blind man's tray,
Then flings the matches back, lit.

. . . Attic, head of the house, dry tank and stored
  memory
Long scraped clean
Where from the skylight, cracked and yellow,
Watch while first she pushed and heaved the bed
  that year,
Out into the snow-crushed garden,
And fumbled raw-eyed numb-fingered with the
  metal cap,
Spattered petrol in a glittering arc
Then threw on the can
And on the match
And stood as if stunned, watching the snow melt
  at her feet,

Trying,
To laugh.

And the child says,   If you have to ask,
                          You can never be told.

      There was no child.
      There was never any child.

Ah, that old napalmic '*whoosh*', Greek fire,
Protestors burning in
The square, trees of smoke rooted in flame
High above the desert . . .

She warms her hands, between wiping her tears.

. . . When the flames were almost out
And brass frame blackened,
She took the last few rags,
And flung them on the beach.

(November 1973)

3.

PROGRESS hardly broke its stride
To deal the city such a blow,
Like a joker off the bottom,
That it flickered and it died
Like a candle caught before the dawn
And rising again as the world spins
Presents itself once more
With all the rest. Like
    Fairground
        Ducks

(December 1973)

Zakalwe's Song

Watching from the room
As the troops go by.
– You ought to be able to tell, I think,
Whether they are going or coming back
By just leaving the gaps in the ranks.
– You are a fool, I said
And turned to leave,
Or maybe only mix a drink
For that deft throat to swallow
Like all my finest lies.
I faced into the shadows of things,
You leant against the window,
Gazing at nothing.
– When are we going to leave?
We could get stuck here,
Caught
If we try to stay too long.
    (Turning)
Why don't we *leave*?
I said nothing,
Stroked a cracked glass,
Found knowledge in the silence;
The bomb lives only as it is falling.

(December 1973)

Sisyphus

Sisyphus eventually wore the hill away
Or ground the stone down to a pebble and
Threw the damn thing up.
Which might be a comforting comparison
With a little eternity too, but
As it is
I can only call you bitch and whore
Thus forcing shut the wound
(Tiny orgasm of pain?)
And through my jaundiced eyes
Contract another disease,
Seduce a further ill,
In hope of curing the first.
– And the eagle gets fed up with liver
– And flies off for different fare

(December 1973)

7.

A blind goat,
Tied to a stake
Driven into the desert
Stretches out its slight
Circumference
And determines
Mountains do not exist.

Einstein's fibre with the
Rest, one day, will
Snap
But pride, or a sense
Of accomplishment
Will be an irrelevance.
From age,
Wear,
Or indifference
The rope may part,
But not from the goat
Having the sense to turn back
And bite it.

(April 1973)

Skull

There is a skull beneath the skin all right,
But beneath the bone
A brain.
And though the hard
Outlives the soft
In the reckonings of decay
That hardness too in dust's betrayed
While that other can, and can choose to
Leave Changes
– And one of those isn't discarding the grain and
Milling the chaff

(May 1973)

9.

Hellfire, brimstone, torture, doom
An etcetera of presumed
Catastrophe.
A sloughed-on mantle of
Indulgent guilt.
    Meanwhile, a certain lack
Of activity in prayers offered
For the souls of slums, a dearth
Of psychoanalysis for those enjoying
Malnutrition, drought, bilharzia
And so on
    (Not to mention real torture)

An old, worn, tawdry set of sins to be called
Original
And not so different
From our touted, screened distractions;
The sapping trivia of our franchised fantasies:
Scum cheap, remorselessly monetised . . .
    Hellfire, brimstone, torture, doom
– An engaging little masochism
But ultimately

    A frivolity.

(May 1973)

Ozery's Song

We are nothing,
Who crawl upon the surface,
Unseen from these heights,
Diffused by distance
Baffled by, frustrated by
Our little, little scale.
    (These the girl's thoughts,
    Suspended from the limitless,
    Carried through the braking air
    Rushing yet still yet . . .)
Ants would be hyperbole,
We have less sense of mass.
The people look like, we look like, are
Nothing.
Only in the darkness are we, conglomerated, seen;
Lights forever outnumber, infinitely outnumbered.
    (These the girl's thoughts,
    Denigrating all,
    From a vantage high
    Procured by, technology)

SSSSSHHHH, goes the jet.

(May 1973)

Hesitation

'We are still strangers as we sleep,
You and I
And all our intimacies
Those hours ago
Make it only more so.'

– It is an old cry, I suppose
Knowing
We have shared bodies
Wondering
Have we shared minds,
And right now I feel more close
To those of my own sex
Who too have lain and wondered so
Than I do,
Lady,
To you.
And I feel I am no longer me
But *a* man, with
A girl
        (Dichotomy; should I call me boy
Or you woman?)
And wonder, perhaps uneasily,
Had you woken first,
What later thoughts
My sleep
Might have raised in you.

You sleep on, oblivious.
– Probably the wiser course.

Another age might have caused some pious
Guilt in one of us at least,
Yet prisoners of one time though we may be
I feel this closer, now, to all other ages,
And all this sexuality.
Our nearly love,
Only
A time machine

. . . Yet it remains, remains yet,
And still I wonder
Do we share thoughts?
Have we shared thoughts?
And if we do,
And if we have,
Was the only one,
This?

(July 1973)

Outward Siege

Comely pleader
But the blow falls anyway
'I happen to bel—'
'Maybe I'm just an old fo—'
'I know it's not fashionable to be—'
The man with his legs
In the air against the wall
Lapping at his shit dribbling back down
(One day the Good Scientist
Made everybody's dream come true
And the next morning the last
Couple put each other against the last
Wall and sho—)

By baleful book, you tore away
The truth to reveal a lie, then tore
Away the lie to reveal the truth, then tore
Away the truth to reveal a lie, then tore
Away the . . .
'Look closer' says the man
And you look closer,
And see 'the' and 'a' and
Claim that and won't believe
A smiling refutation, yes but no,
As disappointed as the cow's
Back legs, still a step behind

Maybe your Idea created
All then turned away to
Other things, forgetting already,
Saying (hand like a match waved out)
'But seriously . . .'
Or left the final tablet
On the mountain
Reading
'. . . though of course, that's only my opinion.'
Hoho, how we laughed, you and I,
Poking out each other's eye.

'Oh, I think we live our lives
On different levels'
– Sure, one foot in, one foot out
– Of the gutter, limping existension.

'You were my hero.'
'Me?'
'Yes, you were my hero,
I worshipped you,
I believed in you
You changed my life
Made me think'
– Never had so low an opinion
Of myself as just after that;
Detest me, throw out all I've
Ever said; deny.destroy.deflate.
Allow me only to provide fit metaphor:
The gripped smoulder dies,
Blowing only sets it glowing.

'Sleep with me'
'Fuck off.'
Divine fencer!
That's the way!
(Love is cheap,
Found anywhere;
But a thorough coldness,
A *growing* climate;
Much much rarer.
The storm before the storm
. . . Any time.)

Who do *I* want to kill?
Oh . . .
– The girl who will lie with you but
Will not undress save in darkness,
– Those who oppose me, acting
Where I react, consider while
I do, accept where I refuse,
Speak while I listen, like
Us, yes?
No. I want to kill no one. You;
Prove what you want:
Creation destroys
Chaos,
Destruction creates
Wreckage
(For every reactionary . . .)
And so saying,
And so giving,
The reactor a speaking part,
Do something
Unsymbolic.

Say, then,
That we are
Ash from the fire's true life,
Diamonds in life's forming pressure,
Lights like suns in the darkness of eternity,
Quick-drying sperm from some god's wet dream
And so on and so on
And more of the dissimilar;
A copy of an interpretation of a translation
Of some passionate indifference
'I hear you're funny, say something funny'
'No'
(She laughs, and I listen contentedly
To the sound of my knuckles
Crunching into mine own teeth.)
– Oh well, said my mentor,
Better luck next time.
– Oh good, I said, relieved.

Lastly, the metaphor
With which I shall conclude.
It is a relativistic explanation
Of reality accounting for the
Ease with which opposing dogmas
Are held and upheld:
Mirror, rainbow (reality),
Different angles,
        "   colours (dogmas);
All else;
One   colour;
   "   place;
Don't understand reflection
(Still barbarians etc.);

Nobody *exactly* same =
    "   "   "   angle.
(The above supersedes all previous
Explanations until further notice.)

'"And that's *Final*! . . . *Maybe*!"'

'*Fuck me!*' (said Buddha from
The pyramid on Calgary), '*If
I'd known it was going
To be this sort of party
I wouldn't have come.*'

    'Sleep with me.'
    'Oh, all right.'

   . . . There . . .

(December 1973)

The Signpost at Midnight

This one
Lying here,
Dead beauty
On red snow strewn
(Oh, I agree, absurdity
Of over-romanticism,
But reality embraces all)
Yes,
This one;
She
– She was of our patterns
(And a needless sacrifice
Oh and the horror and futility
Of horror and futility, ahem)
And if cells we are
– Locked in a whole
Yet with it locked within us –
Then as much was she
Like you or me
And as deserving
One assumes . . .
However,
This one,
She was . . .
She was like one I loved,
If memory serves,
I am not sure;
Dead she gives

Too long a time to look
And like a printed word
Over-examined,
Loses meaning
And disuniting parts
Confuse.
Indeed, we do not always gaze
So long on one love's face
That its imprint lives on still
Faithful
While they or oneself
Is not.
Still
This one
Is not her,
But resembles only,
And anyway
Maybe I'm wrong
And I have never loved
Perhaps so:
Perhaps the memories of love
– Including its lessons of course –
Would be the finally important thing,
The end
To the means of love
(Vague sounds help; one mutters)
And I wonder;
She,
This one,
Was she wise?
Could she judge?
While . . . while that black foam
Lapped a living brow (ah!)

Did she learn her lessons?
Could she discern and decide?
Did she intuit
What others needed told?
Who knows,
Who knows,
And how can we presume to answer
From within our fascination
By the stroke of that cold skin
Or the touching of that hair?
Yes; that frozen inky flood,
Sable breaker on a beach of snow
Checkered vermilion winding sheet . . .
My apologies;
Dead women,
Young, defeated,
Beautiful and tragic
Out on the snow
Like this one,
Fascinate me.
. . . But turning again
I wonder
. . . Could some hardy necrophiliac
Still squeeze some thirteenth-hour pleasure
From this so elegant frame
Twice hardening
In death
And cold?
Could some scavenging girl
Snap off those perfect fingers
For the little jewels
Encircling
But trapped?

Could some hound
A few months hence
Lope off with happy slobber
And bury all the bones of her,
Consume that marrow,
Salivate upon
That finely reared calcium,
And nudge with a sloppy jowl
These sad remainders
To grave scratched
Like a shallow wound
Within the tender earth?
. . . Good god what shit!
'The tender earth'!
What artful nonsense!
Here she lies
A what-billionth, trillionth
Part of all the globe's totality
A nothing,
A dead ember,
An ash speck, returning to the fire
Only as much as you or I
– If that –
And yet what absurd praise I heap upon her
    frozen head.
. . . But then,
One is not the planet,
One is what one knows,
Shut for a too-short for ever
Within a bone prison
Size of a smallish cooking pot
(Peep inside your helmet sometime, my friend,
And behold the universe)

So we can know no wholeness
No completeness
No union or reunion
Except that based on, tied to, anchored against
That singularity.
. . . Ah; my digressions breed, multiply . . .
'This one'
Yes, this one
A dead female
About thirty
Prone, on new snow on a firm base
Who may or may not be the one I've heard of,
A whispered reputation
A name in my mind
A few memories and this visual cue
A remnant like an island in
A drowned caldera
And us here to witness with
Some savage mercy, half unfelt
Just:
Was person, now corpse;
Fit précis, but too tight
(If it is her then they say
She had more lovers than years
From the age of twenty
And that her greatest ambition
Was to have a war named after her . . .)
But all goes,
All consumes and is forgotten
All forgets and is consumed
. . . I would say they don't make them
Like that any more,
If I was certain

That they ever did.
– Still, there's a thing;
How will she be remembered?
This . . . left-over:
Villain, martyr, heroine, innocent?
– A gauntlet run,
Run across a gentle cheek
To wipe a tear away –
How?
No matter, no doubt,
No matter.
She was
She . . . was
That much is and was enough.
　　So,
There we are:
Her epitaph,
Her funeral oration
Before the drifts of life's continuation
Slip over her,
And the wind winds sheets of sleet about.
– I hope the one who killed her
Will be not pleased tonight
But perhaps in some oiling act
Of post-causal supplication
Before that metallic alterer
Guilty of this before us, accessory
Inducing the act
Will of a sudden
Pause, and . . . to . . . Oh,
What the hell;
If at-all-flown thought he has,
If he remembers it,

Or even ever knew,
He'll reflect more like
– And in spite of me –
That of course the trigger's caught
By some so cunning plot
(And so well wrought)
And by all means the bombs remain
In their bays, becalmed by a refrain
And yes the falling knife is paused
Held back by some remembered clause
Too much a quoted scene
For the pouncing cat's momentum
And meaning
Saves us from bumping into our reflection . . .
Or not.
Who knows.
Not I.
     Though perhaps . . .
However; I come too late
And besides; I am as he.
(And – quietly now – I am as she.)
     This one . . .
Was new coals to an old fire,
A too-fine line drawn too late,
A whisper garbled by the too-soft lips
And we are dust, that stay?
Yes; dust, ambitioned to crush
Questions, jealous of the order
Spilled blood
Anxious for the fray.
Who, finding what we fear,
Deny the thing,
And not the fright of it.

For ever provisionally,
Infinity claustrophobed
And, pleading for the ending song,
In more and more resplendent form
Until the exhortation itself . . .
Yes, you guess.
    Goodbye, sweet lady,
Unresponding catalyst
For an unworthy dabbler
In life and war and art;
My comrades and I salute you
And beg your last forgiveness,
For ours was the fight, I feel,
And all you and your privileged kind
But gave us enough rope,
With which, sad to say
(But ending now)
– We hanged you.

(January 1974)

Extract Solenoid

(Missing)
And peeping from the wrecks
We watch the guns copulate,
Flickering raps of cordite ecstasy
And embarrassed cases labelled
'Don't leave this lying about in . . .'
Withdrawing again, letting the
Shards fall back we retreat
Into the gloom
Silent at all we have witnessed.
Only later do you whisper
'Have they taken over the world?'
'Only the biosphere.'
'Oh.'
Tender fool . . .
You girls must stick together
With the exception of your legs of course
While we men deal with the problem.
Already our chief weapons expert
(Missing)

(January 1974)

18.

Displeased with all
The blind men touching it
Up, fondling and
Prodding its
Skin, tail, trunk, legs and tusks,
The beast tramples them all to death
And resumes its work
Composing a treatise on reality.

(January 1974)

Metaphormosis

The bird is a metaphor for freedom,
The bird of freedom.
The book is a metaphor for life,
The book of life.
The tide is a metaphor for armies advancing,
The tide of the advancing army.
The fish is a metaphor for guerrillas,
The guerrilla is a fish.
The unexploded bomb is a metaphor for
    situations,
The situation is like an unexploded bomb.
The cooking pot is a metaphor for society,
Society is a cooking pot.

So the bird shat on the book which
Was washed clean by the tide through
Which the fish swam until it hit and
Detonated the unexploded bomb, throwing
It into the cooking pot where I cooked it
And handed it to you saying
'But look, we're only scratching the surface.'
And you said
'Yes, but from the inside.'

(January 1974)

19.

'The church's windows
Are deepest red
Glass stained on purpose,
Spoiled for effect,
Presenting one dogmatic stillness
In a crude imitation of life.
Chained to history,
Locked in their metal grid,
They are bound by the limits of a dead age,
Sieving the light
Through a colandered grail;
Telling no outward truth at all,
But forcing a cloistered introspection,
A strained account
Red as any heretic's blood,
From a Book as cooked
As any suspect witch.
Galileo Galilee
(Very nearly)
Shattered the church's crystal infirmament,
Yet the windows remain, amassing grace,
Debased and debasing
What should have been the morning's light,
Making all the stones bow down
And face the east.
Transvestment transepts;
Abscessed apses lapse into obsess;
Papal bullshit, knave, Deus

Off the bottom of the pack.
And a slandered Jew
(Unclean of course,
Probably missed by the showers)
Saying
"Jesus Christ . . . already?"
– It isn't your light,
– It didn't cross eight minutes of nothing
To smack your blinkered little *chosen* eye
And justify a fiction.'

'. . . Isn't this just a dig at religion?'

'If that means exhuming it, yes.'

(January 1974)

Love Poem

1/ Serene
2/ In a world full of troubles
3/ i.e. Doing nothing about it.

(April 1974)

Equivocal

Allow me
To make it all perfectly clear
– The sun-filters on the telescopes of your thought
To crystallize it for you
– The blood-of-your-heart-of-your-mind
To shed some light on it
– The germinating bulbs of your soul
To put it neatly, this prospect for chaos
– I am into destruction and out to destroy

Told I have no business, I capitalize
Told to love or leave, I fuck
Told to mind my own, I own your mind.
My aim. Is your point blank faces
My target: the bull of whatever bitchy dogma.
(You believe in a conspiracy?
– Very well, I am part of it, regardless)
And I hit you, right between the ideals.
No warning
– The vast is not measured by the minute
No extortion
– The price of the ride is the warfare
No analysis
– I set out to upset, not set down.
Only occurrence
And the indivisible action of the I
Only doing
And no retreat but onward

Only action.
So know me for what I am not
And that way only comprehend.
Think of me only through repression
And that way only understand.
Meet me by avoidance
And that way only realize
My ambition.

So no more lessons, no more mores;
Change come quickly, it or me
For both mean relativity,
And we'll be back to square forty-six, a
Gain?

(April 1974)

Firing From the Hip –

A.

Then ignore us, as sweat that rises glistening
On the troubled brow of Such Times,
As clouds that form from nothing visible
To inundate a twist of air with substance,
And say we are a broken promise
A tangled threat,
A lie.
But when you fall, we rain.

(May 1974)

B.

You have turned me on a quiet, creamy spit of
    stars
You have thrown me like a leaf before the storm's
    eye
You have broken me over a dark world of sound
You have split me like a cheap brick.
I stammer what names, urge some terms,
Protest a guilt and nurse a little private self-
    regard . . .
But you remain coming,
Like some vast escaping fire,
And I, razed, fall.

(May 1974)

I & II

A dog, an old bitch, walks in the night's cold
   shadow light.
Cold shadow light, half blue, and clouding eyes,
   milky;
Why prowl, old dog? No wolf you, no predator;
Meat from a can.
Still, under a grey blue light and padding,
Round and round the furniture in a room,
Quiet but for the speaker, the set speaker,
Dark but for the cold shadow light,
Cold shadow light of the set.
You are in a cave where you see only reflections
And have none of your own.
What shadows are they, dog? No matter to you;
They are light from a dark screen,
A rounded-off rectangular face, phosphorescing
   lines,
To show us the dark side of our minds.
     Later, dog, I looked from a lit room to where a
       moon was,
Sifted through the gantries and the arches,
Swollen through the dark metal structures
Of a huge bridge vast above over a steep black
   roof.

The moon lit up the going clouds and made the
    bridge
A silhouette. People slept above me.
The thick stone arch above, high on the bridge's
    deck,
Was the entrance to a dark, metal, open cave.
– I watched until my breath made a corona on the
    window
Of the moon in a cloudless sky,
Then let the curtains fall back.

II

Beaches are, we know, places where the sand is
    wiped clean.
The people will write, the sea erase. Old
    footprints, old
Tracks, names, patterns, love messages, pledges,
    jokes; vows
        A cold day, windy; grey waves breaking on
        tarnished sands.
Walking tactics. Two old people going before,
One of us always trailing behind,
One always to the side;
No convergence, speaks the mind, no convergence;
We walk the invisible tracks of tact, and precious
    coyness.
(These are ruts of age, you know; once it was not
    so.)
        A giant wood wishbone she finds, and cries, hair
        blown,
Marching at the sea, 'I divine water!'

43

I walk by, smiling, make the wishbone joke,
She sets the arch down at water's edge, and it falls.
We found an arm-thick length of rope,
Probably from where the cranes scratch at a dour
    sky;
Jokes. Jokes about the rope. One or two; I can't
    remember.
A piece of tar, like dogshit, sticks to my shoe.
I wipe it off on the grass, unseen.
        The distant city   over the water
Is flattened by a grey fleet of clouds.
        Back again, we found the closed miniature
            railway.
I found a thin piece of track ripped up against the
    fence.
The rails strained at the sleepers, wanting different
    ways.
It was frail. I held the tracks in one hand, could
    have
Snapped them, with two.
A minute later, and above us on the banking,
    through fresh leaves,
At first just the diesel noise, a clattering of wheels,
A rumble and our two heads raised,
A real train comes.
        We have acted child-like;
Wanting ride on little train, all closed down, track
    torn up.
Now we laugh
For the real one carries flats stacked high;
Sections of track.
We used to wave to the people . . .

The air grows cold. The narrowing path forced
        us together,
And we talked pleasantly enough. But now
The air grows cold, and the old people turn back.
We follow.
        The dog trampled in a dirty stream,
Mean trickle draining the car park,
And gets its feet muddy.
You, you hid behind a tree, the dog could not find
        you,
Turned three times, sent back, still could
        hardly . . .
But you came round, laughing, made to box its old
        ears, laughing.
I don't want it,   I don't need it,   I won't feel it.
It's an old love, an infection much too old, far too
        recent,
It was just a stage, a blind tug from a foggy place
Where horns from the river sound and the sun is
        red all day.
– Do not stir up that fresh young decay,
Do not disturb what I have exiled in myself;
It was an infatuation, it was just an infatuation
And there is no convergence at all.
        We'll go back now; the cold easterly uncombs
        my hair
And tangles yours. The air grows cold for old
        people,
And there are spots of rain.
        'Oh Shenandoah, I love your daughter,
        Away, you rolling river . . .'
The dog makes the seat dirty,
The tearoom is open again but empty,

The rain comes on, goes off again,
And the grey waves crash on the aching sands.

(May 1974)

Routenburn

– One huge roaring
Fills the sky behind me
As I walk back to the road.
The road is off towards the hill,
Lying heavy under the sinking sun,
Which star comes down
Point perfect on the dark crest,
A dying stare, fresh and falling
Over the land's tilt,
A bead-drawing eye
Closed by its swivelling, silent lid.
I plod a road for savages,
A torn path like a ploughed
Then flattened strip,
Routeless strand torn on to the moor,
Leading from drying river
To drifting road.
Here there is a choked stream
Which runs into the dust and the rocks
Are stained. And also a concrete channel, gagged
    with
A thick brack water, still brown and bits of wood
    and
Brick in it.
– The stream flows, arterial,
Invisibly joined by a million ways –
Crevices, stone-spaces, one-drop rivulets,
Occasional trickles and dropping blades –

To the land it crosses and seeps into,
Rippling mirror of its own evaporation.
The sun comes down defiles to meet it,
Amberly, in burns;
The slow fire in our majority of substance.
Now, the stream is dying,
But so presents a poor image;
It will flow again, flood and storm again,
And when eventually there is no stream here,
There will be others, elsewhere.
Or something, or nothing.
For difference changes like the moving lens,
Swelling liquidly until
A focal point
And then, in the same movement, inverted;
   receding,
And when nothing's left, nothing's left.
But I just think all this. The burn,
Regardless, flows on.
– Over it, at the end of the overflow,
A lamb lies; its side
Opened to the air,
Showing a short mat of gut-dirtied wool
Coloured red coloured brown coloured black and
   grey.
Little hooves hide the head
And it is poised above the stream, reduced,
Lying drying and smelling
Between the smart white concrete thighs
Of the constricted gully.
There-there; it is alive with maggots,
And I have seen dead sheep
By this same stream distended,

By gas corrupted,
Bellies swollen,
Pregnant with productive death.
– Ah, that shared talent of ours, that incipient rot,
That profane, that carnal stench,
Steeping a lament for this place
In our stagnant,
Surface,
Tension.
Cynicism in glasses, I whistle and say, 'Well,
I warned you,' and manoeuvring tactfully upwind, step
Through the vee
The fallen gate makes with the fence.
The fence stumbles on a few more paces
Then fails, skewing away,
Trailing wire, posts slanting;
A bend the eye travels to the earth,
Tram-lines rayed to the ground, lying loose.
Close too,
An over-use of violence
Has smashed the square well cover –
It lies tangled in the wire. Just a cheap housing
Of thick bricks,
Leading to rungs and valve wheels
From dark to makeshift light.
But some ridiculous power's flattened it,
Thrown the brick pieces,
Crumbling white-washed flakes
On to the turned-over ground
Like new teeth.
Amused, one doffs one's shades in passing.
(It was a sort of wilderness once

Closed to us, high etc., wild etc.,
And I, alone, came here,
Feeling foreign, abroad, and pleasantly unfamiliar)
– A bird flies over the rough ground in front of me
Its wings
Incandescing against the brown shadow of the hill,
Caught by the sun-rays
Like fingers through a bone-china ornament.
– The track-made ruin heads for the road, blind.
But well it was its own and well you felt at home,
And it was almost cosy
In summer sundowns when the hill-head stood
Free against the shaded sky,
Nearly bright,
Practically clear . . .
– We mostly liquid things buried our life up here,
In fragile imitation of the water's usual cycle
So that, in turning on, it turns back
Upon itself, as in the plant's reverse combustion,
And, through us, returns to returning,
And falls to fall again.
– Precipitation incarnate, we wish to stay the
        same,
As though to stop
The cells' slow death and birth and beat and flow,
As though to stay
Our biped progress, product of our balanced fall,
As though to stem the flow, root out the flower
As traitors to a perfect calm,
Produced by our imagining,
Producing our own image,
And, trying to walk on the water,
Do not even tread it.

'Usquebaugh,' I say, and smile.
– And come to the road,
Unreal boundary on a transient surface,
To find these destroying builders' place
Littered with
Blocks, girders, heaped on earth,
Tidy piles of barbarians' weapons –
Littered themselves with rubber boots
Like a deserted army –
Comic stands turned over at the top lying
In the dust and on the wood and in the piles or
Caught in the hardened waves of mud
By some past heat frozen still,
Themselves fleck-spattered
With dried tears of mud
– The sun shoves lines of light into your eyes.
The wind sounds in the pylons on the hill above
    the burn.
The hill's reduced, wound round with metal, the
    burn,
Dry. The hillside's ploughed for drains,
The valley cut and
Scarred for pipes and ducts and joints,
Connections and pumps and valves,
And the way you knew it would, it's changed,
But wilder now, not less.
The roaring anthem
In the skies
Above the hill
Announces
Battle; the rip of land, the rival seas
And waves of brown and green
Sing conflict; harmony, their mix;

The slabs and rock, girders and grass conspire
A now sleepless, now unresolvable peace, up here.
– All we can is natural, and
Our vital values find their relevance in only us,
As lifelines, links, shackles,
So we are at our least, and at our most absurd
Applying the ethics of such uncertain life
To our own kind
In graceless imitation
Of what was ever, never ours.
For we do try; and try and try;
We synthesize our guilt, beg forgiveness
– And the question – display disclaimers,
Open the closed only to pack more tight,
And loose upon the world our unregulated chaos,
Its twisted threat
Showing off our stasis flagrantly,
Expounding on our desiccation,
Showing us showing;
While reality dusts us duly,
Places on the flux a flow,
And on the shower a shower.
'I'm sorry,' I told the pylons,
'That's just too old an image; that roar,
That old pre-take-off roar. Too old.'
Dust and silence drifted by,
Memoirs of my own boots passing.
– We live by what we think are orgies,
And are only innocent parties.
We stand at the entrance out, the exit in,
    complain,
'Everybody's left, nobody's left.'
And claim to live by absolutes, not paradox,

Our two feet planted firmly –
But not growing
There-there – to stay, to keep, to hold and
    conserve always
We must move, give, alter and adapt in all ways.
Here, here we live on a shifting,
Revolving and wobbling in another revolving,
Going headlong, revolving in expansion in change.
Hence the fortress,
All our systems
And our fears and hopes.
And, with perfect imperfection,
So detesting the change and movement
That we seek such stasis we imagine might exist,
We try to find the unfounded,
And so move, and so give, and so.
– I shake my head, smile, adjust glasses.
Put on helmet, pull up gloves,
Key the machine I straddle,
Ready to go away.
'Too old, too old,' I said. 'I'm sorry, too old.'
– I am just one of the faster-moving things up
    here,
Only a little more independent;
A jumble of sums and products,
And more differentiated than integrated.
– I walk, mindful,
On the mindless land,
And grin knowingly at the idiot sun,
The dumb water,
Imbecile steel,
Moronic earth,
– And none of us jealous.

Skull encased in plastic,
Eyes behind the polarized,
Body clothed synthetically,
I sit on metal, rubber, fuel;
Vain beast visibly
Joined to it all by a million processes –
Cracking, refining, mining, smelting
Forging form in a ferrous shape,
Too glibly named and balanced to be dwelt on,
I think; and smile; and twist
And life – of a certain sort; lasing stopped lazing –
Bursts roaring on this even land beneath:
'Too old, too old. I'm sorry, too old.'
Hill; valley: bright unhuman life,
Hill, valley; textures, colours, motions,
Hill-valley, chain itself once, now cycle still,
Now link chosen for the low way it presents,
Living on, lived off,
Neither awake, neither dreaming; neither dead.
'Too old, too old. I'm sorry, too old.'
– The stream too is a highway:
    And the road flows.
'Too old, too old. I'm sorry, too old.'
– It was never our barbarity,
    We were never what we thought we feared,
    And it was always like this.
Too old
    Too old
      So sorry,
        Too old . . .

(May 1975 and October 1976)

J – an apology

Lady, I have tried to love you less,
And in so trying, I am also tried
As loving, I find you, so too I find myself
Guilty, of loving you.
I have made the attempt of brushing such concern
    aside,
But failed.
– The love I have of you will not be so removed,
For though I had thought it just impression,
A possibly painted thing, thin scrape and scene,
Which I could with ease erase
By only demanding the effort from myself,
I find instead it is a virtual image
A reflection of a truth outside,
Word and substance perfect,
You text; your reality and shape, mirrored, no
    mere texture.
– And trying to rub away that being,
To remove the object of this fascination,
I do not smear or smudge or even darken slightly,
But rather wipe from that smooth glass
The remnants of what dust may there adhere
And with my hand soak up the condensed breath
My existence placed
Between me and my love;
So see you clearer
And more lovely
Than before.

So; self-confounded,
What can I do to love you less,
But try to love you more?

(November 1976)

On The Wrong Lines

Love requires a sharing,
And though it be admitting my defeat,
I'd rather I returned your only relative regard for
   me
Than all my life so love you, one-sided and
   condemned.
Fool, I had thought that seeing you again might
   break the spell,
Like the princess kissing the frog, only
To be left with slime on her lips.
– But the despicable old trick works every time,
And here, through this
Explaining
What can never be more than mine
Or less than yours,
I try – on paper anyway – to share my love.

(November 1976)

Mediterranean

Xerxes exerted, beat and did not beat
The straights.
Instead their sound bayed after him,
Footsteps in his dust,
A water message, a level hiss;
'Hey, Emp; go for gold!'
(Persia will be boycotting this year's
    marathon . . .)

Nearby, soon afterwards,
In Damascene and Pride,
The Strong Man stood and bellowed,
'Me Tarsan, you Jesus, OK?'

Lately, not far away,
At Stalingrad and Kursk,
The rhinos fought it out in the dust.
The scorched ground bloodied under their hooves,
The ants were by the million crushed.
Kulak and painter they rammed and roared
And sang their theme
In two-point harmony:
'Kalinka, Treblinka . . .'

– Man with his dark scythe, he smile in his dark
    cowl, say
'History is on my side.'

Boys, boys, you got the whole thing wrong;
We're the players, not the audience,
The grifters, not the marks;
Get those lights turned back again,
Back out of those gods,
Beat it to the wings,
And tell the Brahmin, Jew and Gentile
'Tough, lads, the plague has spread.'
– Meet me in Ilium,
By the big horse.
Bring a friend.

Pitiless, impartial, the sunlight like
Our brilliant opposite
Downs like scarab-foam.
– And the pyramids sharpen Occam's razor.
(Ah we are the surface age, the age of the veneer,
Here we are the rhinestone age, the frivolously
    pragmatic now.
The more we learn of other times
The less we understand:
How could we accept great Khufu
As monument to a different death
That ends up just the same?
No! It must have a purpose!
– Quickly, think of something –

Waves,
Composed, resilient, cerulean,
Here for the how-many-thousandth time returned,
Lap us lazily.)

Ichorus: RA RA RAA!
    Sol for ever!

Sirs, the tale shrank in the telling.
But never mind,
We've turned the corner.
Like that dude Daedalus said:
'No worries, son; all downhill from here.'

Cradle, cradle, your golden bough broke,
The baby fell, the little children suffered,
The whited sepulchre, Fat Lady, called them,
And crusading they were crucified,
Battered, bartered every side.
Ulysses, the conning, sold them clapped-out boats,
Moses denounced them on a tablet,
Nelson with his carronades,
Rommel using eighty-eights
Caught them in a cross-fire.
Off Beyreuth
A refugee ship ran them down.
By Gaza
The Styx broke all their bones
– But do not think they've gone yet,
No no, they haven't gone yet.
You can see them still;
Their broken bodies litter every map
With letters, contours, figures, lines;
Their contaminating innocence abounding,
Budding Legendary full displayed,
They flock flapping
Like lines of black bunting,
And our rooks

Our dead chicks
Fly home.
And mate.

– Shoo-bop-do-bob
   Hey-hey
   Just lookin for the Ringmaster,
   Lookin for the Ringmaster,
   Yeah just lookin for the Ringleader.

From the Golden Horn to the Pillars of Hercules
They floated on the tide.
Alexandria and Actium
Corregidor and Hiroshima
Saw them washed ashore.
From Barbary to Barbarossa,
Through Suez and Sarajevo,
In Kolyma and Wounded Knee,
Tenochtitlan and SoWeTo
The little corpses dropped.
By the wall,
Under the wire,
At the foot of the pyramid and the service gantry,
In the shadow of the Eagle and the Star
They lie.
In the wake of Black Ship and Missile Cruiser
Container Carrier and Golden Barge
They bob.
Under the wheel of chariot
The track of Centurion and T54
They wait.

Andante!
Andante!
It's just an alighieri!

Isis ICBM, Tarot MIRV, Pisces SALT,
INRI, SPQR, USSA, BOSS,
IMB, KGB, MAD, DMZ, SDI
We
Here born beneath our Sign, The Wall,
We
Hear the same sound everywhere:
'– Can't make an omelette without –'
'– Sink or swim; survival of –'
But ah, you know it's ending,
You surely know it's ending.
The troughs come, waves go,
But the tide is our way only
And all your precious words
Are but the
'– Necessary debris –'
Of your rise and fall,
When through our seeing hands,
Projecting eyes
And mumbled ears
The masks are found to fail
And the strata's by a slip revealed.

For all your power,
For all your proud nomenclature,
For all your stalwart faiths
And pious, catechismic lies,
For all subjects marshalled, uniformed, drilled
And made the same,

For all your taught bigotry and cant
Insisting Type and Race and Difference,
You are but oxen by the oxbows at sunset;
Silt, braiding, outfall;
The ruins of ruins,
The last of the first.

Freeing now,
Prepare to enter the synthetic age,
Formic acid tripping you up.
Steel yourself for negative dreams, and a vision
Of more hearts, souls and minds
Flying a flag the colour of the night.

'Here is the latest score: Saturn 5, Sam 7.'

Hey kids
Shoot your stupid myths,
Kill your cosy faiths,
Fuck your wizened gods;
But no personality culls,
No *Auto-da-Fés*,
No Final Solutions.
The word's just through;
Xerxes and the Spartans are even now,
The rhinos
– Ever phantoms –
Broken ants.
And the Cilician never really changed.

So turn on us now, you blood-dark sea
Before you're poisoned, if you dare
And say 'Sorry, it's all been a mistake.'
It is no good,
It will not wash
– We cannot hear
Because our ears stay stuffed with wax.
– We cannot see
Because our eyes have been put out.
– We cannot wave
Because our hands are nailed.

The shadow-play is over:

– You are powerless.

This is our show now.

(August 1977)

A Word to the Wise

I think we can all join in on this one:
'They aren't ready for the truth.'
But innocence never could lay claim to us;
That beast we invented,
With so much else,
For what we hoped was so,
And took it in the teeth.
Just so it's true
We're never really ready,
And what we should exalt
Instead we quick condemn.
But still we change,
And always it's the truth ahead we aren't ready
    for,
Not the ones that should have killed us long ago;
We're ever on the point of falling,
Never quite up-ended yet.
So to those of you
Who can't see the star for the light,
And would drown the dog to kill the flea,
Consider that it's never enough
To know you're right;
You have to doubt it too.

(August 1977)

Exponential

Evening blitzed a distant edge of hills,
A marking fire of cloud and sky which
Like all things impressing,
Stunning human sense,
Its own scale created
Above the plain.
On a line of wooded cliffs I stood,
And looked away, no stranger to the sight or place
But for this time brief exile,
Mediate between two homes.
– I had turned to watch the darkened East,
An old origin of dull,
When fast from that shadow
A bird raced,
Spilling across my view, left to right,
Drawing my eyes from set to setting,
Filling their unfocused sight
With a silent rush of light increasing,
A within-that-second gradual change
At first believable, the usual thing,
Then quickly to a glorious absurdity
Of impression overloaded,
Surging like a groundburst,
Astonishing in its contrasted strength,
Transfixing that bird, outlined finally
In my swamped sense,
Extant

Elated, charged with intensing force,
While the bird flew on across the roads and fields
    away,
I raised a fist and shouted,
Screamed my own insensate call,
A manic, fit salute, inchoate product
Of a mirror in me,
Twisted like the broken strands
Of river on the land below,
A snakeskin scale reminder,
Jazzed reflection, shining glyph.

But that done,
And slightly nervous of having been heard,
I left
And took the paths
From that vantage down
To my place in things again.

And though the echoes, light and voice
In every land live on
As challenge, password, vow,
Expression of a vulgar sanity responding,
And though the lesson every day
Reflects, rebounds, insists return,
Is there for all with mind to see,
It is that mirror-snare within
That resounds its subject longest,
And jealous of its captured glimpse,
Draughts the bird aloft,
From time to time.

(August 1977)

Spin-Off

How often does the thing need said?
'Thou shalt not kill.
Except, of course . . .'
Let us go back to nature then,
Attempt even to imitate the feral,
And so watch the charade
Take on a further irony
Cell
And diode
Obey the same laws.
But in our blindness
– Seeming subservience or imagined mastery –
We fail to match velocities,
And from the dais of arrived
Observe the engines of Newtonian moralities
Leak their sapient fat.

(August 1977)

(Remains Of)

Gold on blue the castle,
Wreck of stone above a pendulum sea,
Galleon on its waves of barley;
Another explorable thing.
And so I climb,
Take a twisted echo of its steps
Like some hollow-lightninged stump
To another storey in the evening air.
A gull
On a nest
Faced me when I raised my eyes.
It moved its head slowly,
As though to see better
Drawing with one unsudden bead.
I ignored it, took in the view.
– The bird rose, turned,
Shat yellow-green along the stones
And flew.
I clambered the short distance,
Smiled down at the nest and egg,
Then picked that reptile-remnant up
And threw it down, cracking on a grassy floor.
– The egg had been long lifeless,
Cracked, the inner membrane stained,
Dried solid.
The bird . . . well, the bird could know no better;
The dumb will always nurse the dead.

(August 1977)

041

My lady's voice on the phone
Like an electric thread of silk
Drawing me back through night's dark maze
To a stormy city
A handful-hundred miles away.
'There's thunder,
Can you hear it?'
I hear
Something too fine, too balanced
To be called tangle,
Too wisely innocent of plans, devices
To be named weave.
I press the plastic closer,
Try to bring her nearer.
'Can you hear the thunder?'
But the gale is drowned,
The rain hushed,
Thunder quieted.
She speaks,
And a gentler force
Overwhelms all of them.

(August 1977)

23.

Real city, hive of memories
I drove you through,
Dividual force
In your storm-washed fastness.
Remembered thought strung me through the
    labyrinth,
Passing lost places, my lived-in ruins
(Here I walked back,
The small hours like change
Rattling in a torn pocket.
I saw a silent swan on black water glide
And knew that what I hoped had just begun
Was over long ago)
– I pressed on then, as before,
And left the city well behind.

On my return, again by you,
I traced a recent tag,
The young battle-place,
Boarded, prosaic, wetted
(Here I joined but did not join,
Here we won but did not win)
– The car bears on, oblivious and sure,
And the city,
Its little escapades relived, forgotten,
Is surrendered to the driving rain.

(August 1977)

I to I

Confess I must
A certain love of turning things about,
Of standing them on their feet,
Of setting them on their heads again.
– An obsession with the literal
Rather than the literary,
With the apposite,
Not the opposite.
Excuses, fast and thick
But slow,
And thin
Leap: 'Well, everything's so mixed up
That negatives are just as . . . in fact probably a
    bit –'
But really it's reaction;
Tic, knee, jerk, gag,
A trick for cheap laughs
Bought at the expense of something real
Unsaid.
And all I hear
Are the words ringing in my mouth:
'I suspect the boy has hidden shallows.'

– Inside every showman
Is a bore waiting to get out.

(August 1977)

Irregular

Let me be the heretic:
Our history is too full
Of exciting opportunities
For young men with ambition
    (I'll list you no lists: prepare your own)
Prepared to work hard under strict discipline
    (Excuse you no excuses)
For substantial rewards.
– I'd rather be irrelevant when they're good
Than bad when they're bad,
And better my own coward
Than a key position
In an expanding
    (Lack of)
Concern.

(August 1977)

Somewhere Near the Snow Line,

Where the sun moved shadows cold as cloud,
Where the burnings reflected, distant, silent,
On our lakes and lands,
Somewhere there, in trees or rocks they came,
Found her, took her, killed her.

Alive, my damaged limbs are bound,
Shrouded like a partial death.
Being repaired, city and palace
Stay stretched about with wood and rope;
Splints for dreams, and airy skeleton,
A scaffold like a squandered longing,
Caught, hung out in the rain to dry.

These streets, the hollow yards, full pits I see.
Shattered trees, by blast debarked,
Smooth wood like flesh, like bones,
And a ripped-up fallen-down bridge.
– A dog, run over by a rubble cart
Whimpers from a culvert,
Cannot be tempted out.
– Even broken, indisposed and in retreat
I should have chased,
Roared into the mountains' sullen weight
Rescued, or in death finding,
Revenged.
I would have covered her in my colours,
Raised a graven emblem

On a stranglehold of snowfield
And knelt and wept, on sword or gun.
('Here boy, here boy.')

Her skin was bone-pale,
Like alabaster pinked by evening light.
Her hair was black as polished coal,
Her eyes blackbird bright,
Her voice deft enough to persuade
A noise-disturbed cornice to change its mind
And stay, hang; not fall.

The birds bunch on burned branches,
Leap, fly off, darkening the sky.
The last leaves fly in their wake,
As though envious.
The mountains silt with snow,
The clouds curdle, thicken every day,
All grows shaded,
My bones knit.

– When I am older,
When I am all things done,
Stiff as wood, bulked as stone,
Hard as fire, grey as snow,
Then shall I tell how I loved her,
Make a grand and unrequited thing of it,
Explain it, embellish it a little,
Repeat it rather too often,
And make my listeners sigh
While my old frame aches for all that's gone.

I stand
At the glacier's foot
Where the trapped, the frozen always come.
But find no crystal caves, no brilliant blue or
    white,
Just dirt and torn-out stone, pocked ice,
Grey and brown,
Receding stumps like teeth ungummed.
I look for bodies unfrozen; none.
I say, 'It's like Time.'
But even my triteness finds no echo here.

Turn away.

Hobbling back, I see the dog, dead,
Legs tied to a post,
Skinned in one quick de-gloving movement
By a thick-set woman with a pocked face.
The sound of it echoes yet in me, may never
    silence.
I retched at the time, and another dog, skinny,
    shivering,
Limped over, licked up the sick while I wiped my
    lips and cried.
New orders waited on me; we retreat again, fall
    further back.

Where did you go my golden age?
– All choked away to nothing.

I loved you like
Like . . .
But nothing comes.

Birds, leaves, mountains, sky
My bones.

All grows shaded,
And another stupid dream gets its neck cut.

(September 1977)

Same Sea

Awash.
Between one
And its opposite.
– Merely a matter of values.

That bright, incisive line,
Reconsidered
Becomes

An ultimate softness.

The shore
This shore
– A curve
A property of straight lines.

Perfect closeness,
Untouching intimacy,
Subsurface and above;
An indeterminacy
Far from what we hope and fear,
Still with us in our exile, searching;
A torted querulousness,
A silence waiting to be heard,
Its import
Though not quite here or there,

Though round a corner, just out of sight;
With.

And the same sea washes all of us.

(January 1978)

Jack

Night bus to Glasgow;
The end of a greater trip.
– A clamorous bunch of motley proles
Taken by the old roads north,
Stopping at neoned stations on the way;
Islands of formica in the dark.
The old man in shiny trousers,
The scruffy hitcher,
The young mother and crying child,
The elderly lady with *People's Friend*,
The two lads with yesterday's *Sun*,
All carried through this damp November night,
A tangle of our separate lines
For as long as we listen to the same gear change,
All watch the sodium vapour lights
Of distant towns go by
And shift our knees to ease the same ache.
– I was sitting beside an old man;
Thin limbs and thick glasses,
And worn tweeds that looked too heavy for his
    slightness.
Eventually, as I tried to sleep,
Legs wedged against the seat in front,
He started talking, asking where I was going,
What doing, where I'd been.
I sighed and talked.
My name was Iain, his was Jack,
And somehow we started on Science;

He asked how people could really tell
That things were so-many-million years old,
How anyone could say what came when and
    where.
He couldn't understand; he was a Christian,
And the Bible seemed much more sensible.

And Christ, dear reader, what could I do?
Oh, I made the lame, half-hearted try;
I told him all was linked,
That those same laws
Of physics, chemistry and math
Which let him sit here, in this bus,
With that engine, on that road
Dictated through the ages
What was so.
Carbon 14 I mentioned, its slow and sure decay,
Even magnetic alignments, frozen in the rocks
By the heat of ancient fires;
The associated fossils, floating continents,
Erosion, continuity, change.
But from the first tired syllable, in fact before,
I knew it was pointless, stupid, a waste.
I talked, and as I talked, switched off.
And somewhere back
Of all this well-informed layman stuff,
Something a little more like the real me listened,
And studied Jack's glasses.
– They were old, with heavy dark-brown frames;
The glass was thick, and thick with dust.
Dandruff, dead scales of old flesh, hairs
Cemented there by grease or stale sweat,
And even if the prescription wasn't years ago

Exceeded by his dying sight,
The grime – the personal, impersonal debris
On those old, scratched lenses –
Smothered a sight too poor to catch the fact
Either from inside those frames
Or out.

He took in nothing.
My throat got sore.
The borders came,
And soon he was met by his sister
In some dismal little rain-soaked town.

I sat in the bus going on,
Watched the lights, red yellow white,
Their smooth but bitty echoes
Refractions
In the spattered hemispheres of clinging rain,
And through the same glass
Saw a watery sun appear.

City, we could do nothing for each other.
Not one seat, but an age
Divided us,
And we get what?
Him
– A perhaps interesting chat
With a typically know-it-all youth
As yet, no doubt, unwise to the world's down-
  grinding ways,
And a head full of fashionable scientific nonsense.
Me

– An encounter almost encouraging in its
   hopelessness,
An experience just as I would have expected.
And never mind what he switched off to,
What he thought of my long hair,
Or doomed, one-sided materialist views;
I got that perfect, pathetic image,
Those glasses, thick on thick,
That I wanted to take from him, wipe, give back,
That self-created dust, so dimming, so destroy,
To somehow help (but I did not do it)
To let him see (but I could not do it)
To do some good (as above).

But no,
The thing gives what it can,
And between the essence
And its metaphor
As those two ages, briefly proximate,
– There is no congruence.

(March 1978)

'Slight Mechanical Destruction'

Zakalwe enfranchised;
Those lazy curls of smoke above the city,
Black wormholes in the air of noontime's bright
   Ground Zero;
Did they tell you what you wanted to be told?
Or rain-skinned on a concrete fastness,
Fortress island in the flood;
You walked amongst the smashed machines,
And looked through undrugged eyes
For engines of another war,
And an attrition of the soul and the device.
With craft and plane and ship,
And gun and drone and field you played, and
Wrote an allegory of regress
In other people's tears and blood;
The tentative poetics of your rise
From a mere and shoddy grace.
And those who found you,
Took, remade you
('Hey, my boy, it's you and us knife missiles now,
Our lunge and speed and bloody secret:
The way to a man's heart is through his chest!')
– They thought you were their playing,
Savage child; the throwback from wayback
Expedient because
Utopia spawns few warriors.
But you knew your figure cut a cipher
Through every crafted plan,

And playing their game for real
Saw through their plumbing jobs
And wayward glands
To a meaning of your own, in bones.

The catchment of those cultured lives
Was not in flesh,
And what they only knew,
You felt,
With all the marrow of your twisted cells.

(March 1978)

Caucasian Spiritual

'Qhwai-Xkhwe, little friend,
Is all we are;
Vex or cave,
Real or virtual,
Our brief *journée*,
My lensman,
Is just a moses trip,
For cradle might as well be tomb,
All is flow and monotone change,
And our attempts at meaning
End up the day as rushes,
Never make the big picture.

Look about you
At this moment in time.
An on-going situation's what you see;
A non-functional viability interface,
A horror scenario
Of dreamt-of disproportions,
As though the unthinking
Thought the thinkable at last
("Emmanuelle can't.
  But her man can.")

Ours is an age of Megalives,
Our spaceship planet a Free Fire Zone,
Our progress a Reconnaissance By Fire
Into a Meaningful Dialogue with our fate.

"Hey everybody! New *Cluster Bomb*'s arrived!"
(Sorry, had to destroy the set . . .)

Myself I think this strange construction
Must be but an acquired distaste,
The track retraced,
However out of synch
Retains some logicality
Wherever it is stopped or slowed;
The flickering image,
Spastic, neurasthenic, *petit mal*,
Is revealed by sideways motion,
Ever skidding to a start.

Play it again, Spam:
"Take me but leave the girl."
"It's no good; I can't go on. Leave me here."
Qwertyuiop ARMS,
"But sir!"
Cdefgab CHARMS.
"That's an order, soldier."
"Yes sir!"
"There's still one thing I don't understand –"
"Oo! How can I ever repay you?"
"Come out of there, Flannegan, you're surrounded."
"Oh, I'll think of something."
"We'd have done it, too, but for those pesky kids."
"Come in and get me, copper!"
"Well, I ain't never bin much one for religion,
  ma'am, but . . ."
"Go on; give me an excuse to kill you."
"How do I know I can trust you?"

"As surely as though your finger were on the
   trigger."
"You don't."
"It's no good sir! Clichés aren't stopping it!"
"Say that again . . . That's it!"
– Ah; so near,
And yet,
So close.

Learn to control your Zeta rhythms,
Become yourself,
Find real satisfaction,
Join the provisionals,
World Peace Through World Trade,
Thirs a cirtin quite sistisfiction
Abit pitting away the Blix,
Go on touch it go on it won't no harder christ
   that's . . .
With this ring I do thee –
– AWW, FUCK!

Earth earth my earth
We're just your little children,
Don't you know me?
Can't you hear me?
Am I just another mouth to starve?
Jeez, I'd walk a million miles for one of your
   similes;
Speak to me.

How long have I thought I was God?
Why, ever since I was first thought of.

– You and me, these teeming tribes,
Their dreary lives and loves.
Such sad descriptions,
Desecrations,
What's it all but Shootout Territory,
Anyway?
An unsound stage a one-take wonder,
Something the second unit did
With sloppy continuity.
No one even agrees what we're making here;
Is it Malice In Wonderland,
Or Pogrom's Progress?
– Help me search for meaning,
For *meaning*, you gibbous dissembler,
You dull star;
I didn't do all this for nothing.

(You know the moon could always see,
And with its cold and stony heart
Gave up going round,
Settled one face to you,
Slowing down, coming back,
A slow-slow oscillation,
A shaking of its head, finally,
As if it knew.)

– This was just the first draft, honest.
You wait . . .

Okay;
Hit me with the re-frain!
– The end justifies the means,
The end justifies the means,

The end justifies the means,
The end mustifies the jeans,
The jeans end the mustifies,
If the meanies send the just,
Ends the jean must, i.e. if the,
Jim, see that he stun side fen,
It's just that he dies, men; he fane,
If Enid's the just, mean thee?
Adeeeeefhhiijmnnssstttu.
– The end justifies me, thanes;
The dust is thine, aeeefhjmns,
If this ends, aeeeehjmnsttu.

Well,
C'est la mort,
It matters not,
It was all a long joke anyway
. . . Repeated sections . . .
. . . Same thing happening . . . a
Long Involved Explanation
To while the time away;
Mere *badinage*
For ages minus 4004 and upward.
– And even if you could have known,
My little ball of dust,
You never would have.

Earth, you're only deep on the surface;
Inside,
You're shallow to the core.'

(March 1978)

A Glass of Water

Under this unhurried night,
The new year's sharp raw edge,
In this assemblage; bricks, windows, steel,
– An unexpected birth
A strange-thing-come-to-pass.
. . . We drink a glass of water,
Watch our shared sweat drying.
There is: the silence of the passing trains.
There are: a few hours, slipping.
And the tangent feel,
– A world beneath us.

Sleepless touching,
Touch astonished,
And dawn,
Like a slow white hand come cupping
Us and all,
Holds us here,
Like this glass of water,
Consumed.

So I watch that singled light come streaming
Through hair, through water, glass,
And I see I am reduced,
Used perfectly,
And grasped.
– I am another tumbler,
Another, falling, chaser.

I touch your lips
And vanish.

(January 1979)

Resumé

We know there are two voices in this thing,
Two voices talking in a darkened room,
Speaking trying to share
What is already shared.
Those lips with air
As soft as skin, or more
Caress
An occupying space,
A filled-full understanding,
Body-breath.
The ears,
Whorls, caves,
Cradled in that hair, this arm
Accept,
Combine with waves in transit
Going homing through the cells' small shocks
To make a final circle.

One thought
To another thought,
Through voices in a darkened room
They revolve around
Two places
Where this is no pain.

(January 1979)

Song for J

Falling, I am raised
To see what's to be seen
Not in a kinder light, but true.
Knowing this,
Shall I worship you and say you are my own?
Shall I say our love can never die?
Shall I name it sacrosanct, divine,
And you an angel, goddess, spirit?
– Dear *amateur*, I'd not debase you so,
Nor what we have devalue
To contract terms and fictions.
You are too much yourself and here
To need my sly comparisons,
And what we share
Is of itself and now
A part of all this change,
And finds its true worth there.
– Lady, that soft skin,
Your bones and mine
Will all be dust
Before another mountain's raised.
No oceans,
Not a river,
Hardly a stream
Will dry
Before our eyes do,
And our hearts.
– But should I love you less,

For such ephemerality?
– I think the more instead.
For our love's in the real world;
Profane and carnal, at times banal,
But in our human sight, sublime.
No greater, but quite different
To dying suns and levelled range compared
We share from our two separate selves
A happenstance understanding,
An unfateful fate,
Designed by, decreed by nothing,
Ungiven, not granted,
But ours the more for that,
The thing no thing can ever learn,
The first and final lesson:
Mortality is a quality of life.

(January–February 1979)

Meniscus

I find myself in love, am told I'm blind,
Losing sight of what I should regard,
Disregarding, in my vagueness,
The usual little niceties.
– But such blindness is concentration,
A focus of all sights to one.
In this the telescope and microscope
Are blind as well,
Bringing one thing closer
To the mind and shining,
Unreal only
In its magnified reality.
And in the eye
The very spot which we call blind
Is where our sight's condensed

The mind is just a greater eye,
The ultimate lens we have,
Myopic, astigmatic, it's what we've got to live
    with,
And this new thing spectacular,
In such a kind assault,
Produces its own image when
We face,
And midway to perfection
The photons mix and pass,
So that there, light lady,

Erratic or erotic, albedo or libido,
We find ourselves, in love.

(January–February 1979)

Spoils

Killed heroes as they join the earth,
With no room left to spare,
Still have some time for soiled recollection
As their spirits hit the air.
Decanted and discounted and recanting,
They can remember
– A hose playing under search-lit water,
Its silent coils writhing.
– The way a certain head was bowed,
Outlined then in firelight.
– How a dawn came up in winter
And stars, campfires, were light-washed out.
– When the smell of crushed grass the battlefield
Invaded; a scent of harvest.
– They see their progress as a fever,
Life an infection, producing
Spasms, sweats and shouts;
For not too long.
– Antibodies disembodied
They know at last
All else to but another knowing
To consciousness is
Inimical
And that their love dies with them,
Not the reverse.

The candle gutters but is not snuffed.
In its failing light no other takes its place.

And mere smoke the debris,
An afterbirth finale,
Shedded, disperses

– By an unholy power,
By itself meaningless,
As senseless as it is implacable
And irresistible, coerced,
They go to their cold ends
Not to be commended or condemned
Nor contemplate a life so stamped with error,
But purely to embrace
That less
Than brilliant definition:
Death as terminator.

(February 1979)

25.

By a timeless movement trapped,
With a touch entranced,
In a word captivated,
Like something caught in amber,
The faceted eye there set,
I live in this strict clarity,
Consider what it represents.
– Talismans of incertitude:
Crowding moons and fragile blooms,
Wings of insects, sighs of fools.
– I talk of half-lives, doubled;
Real time in the core;
A balance at the nucleus,
And say you have a hand in my escapement
– Shout, Got you! and we're free.

(February 1979)

Askance

Versions of the truth disseminated
To the flock like plastic shrapnel,
Getting under the skin of most,
And on the nerves of some.
– Another chip off the old blastoma,
Another symptom;
The bloom and sump of diabetical materialism.
– Come give us your excuses,
Explain why you did what you had to do,
Tell us of your hurting to be kind.
– You talk of
Bloody Sundays, Black Tuesdays,
And all the time you're wasting.
– We'll smile, dissemble,
Case the joint for barricades,
Count the weapons,
Cost the operation
And mutter back meantime
'I believe that's just the way it happened.
I'm sure it's exactly as you say.'

(February 1979)

Revue

Days unstrung by us and spent,
Slattern's litter, wrenched necklace; fallen beads,
Three calm hearts in a fevered corpse,
And history an old man sweeping up.
– Examine all your selves,
Over each logged belief pore;
Make up your mind
(From spare parts)
(That are memories)
Tell me:

– The truth is just a lie
That happens to correspond to the facts.

(July 1981)

Debriefing

On a plane of fatted dust I stood,
A beast alone on others' backs;
A shadow over all the accidental past.
Deep in softness,
Surrounded and surmounting,
The wind came like a flaw,
Wrapped memories and dreams
Around my legs,
And carried on.
– From dark sky come big ship;
Fire and wind, expectable.
Hoist your weapons, tramp lads,
Lids closed from the false wind,
Enter it.
– Wipe them from your eyes,
Spit them from your teeth,
Snort them, prize them;
Turn young backs
On a winter's desolation
And go through pastel shades and filtered air
To shower   rec. soc. and sleep,

And so ignore
(As viral, phallic, a shaft of fire we ride
From this wrung cell away)
– The wilderness inside.

(July 1981)

Capital

Yielding
yields,
Gilded
gilts,
Each
column's
base
Conceals
Dead Bones

(July 1981)

Wealth

Just unjust
Peace – bits
Laws make walls
A classy lesson:
Crimes whisper.
Money talks.

(July 1981)

New

Quiet as snow from a windless sky
Slow as lichen on a scoured stone spreading
By year and through decades
By century and for histories
Minute blossoms prick black wastes
Like bright bubbles
On a nightfall of dark ocean.

Their lives counted in forgotten cities
By millennia and jungles long submerged
Their immensity measured
In splintered parings of degrees,
A detonation of far stars froths up
And scatters from each seeded globe
Their offspring
Like pollen on the wind.

(July 1981)

Thermal

Vultures, pinned to blue,
Hang in the sky;
Flat specimens
On an endless card.
Hooked to the air
In a rising spiral turning
An orb of eye surveys
The carrion possibilities.

(July 1981)

Rannoch I

Pressed on the plain, a line.
In a frozen force of snow
Stilled reams of whiteness, edge to edge,
Beneath a mirror sky, formless and blank,
The train moves.

Diesel from the engine, clattering
In a white-out silence,
Steam from the carriage, wisping
In the clear-air space.

The wheels splash, throwing water, slush,
From covered steel; the train banks,
Moving slow on sunken rafts reburied.
Beyond the dark wood, grimy glass, steam smell,
Deer run, brown startling; hooves flash black.

– I watched the light from the snow-filled moor
Shine on her face through the dirt-flecked glass,
I saw the fields of grey clouds move;
Ponderous, obscure,
Then in carriage's humid warmth,
Shivered
From that surface's cold glow.

(July 1981)

Ken MacLeod
Poems

Erosion

The waves roll like logs into the bay
and splinter, hissing, up the beach.
Violent, even on the calmest day.
God does not know how long they took
to grind these cliffs exceeding small
to a thousand million tons of sand.

The new cemetery on the headland fills
with headstones like hilts in a stabbed back.
The minister stands on slowly shifting hills
and does it by the book: 'Their souls are immortal,
their bodies
rest till the resurrection.'

Their souls are electrochemical
tracks in others' brains. Their bodies
under the sharp, salt-water grass
are earthed.
The Atlantic ignores the land.

(1974)

Uneasy Lies

It's time.
'It always was.'

and wake
at that junction
where trains of thought are
systematically derailed and randomly
shunted: passengers crated away, crates
bellowing for the porter and when it comes
drinking it

in that zone
where surrealism is camera I
(winks)

and flounder in that surf
between dream and reason
battered by cortical waves, dragged
back by undertow
and hear
the triumphant echo of the despairing yell:
'It always will be!'

and wake
remembering only incomprehensible sentences

being passed.

(Winter 1973–74)

Charles Fort

Skulls fossilized in coal; sargasso seas;
frog-showers; flying lights, and coloured rain;
writing engraved on meteorites – all these
and more he could record, but not explain.

Aristotle called theories 'likely stories'
and this man, also, was not deceived:
all his deductions and hypotheses
were tales he went on telling, but no more believed
than he believed that 2 plus 2 make 4.

An abnormal attitude that was completely sane.
Gripped by such facts, how could he set much
    store
in the fragile constructions of the brain?

(Winter 1973–74)

Faith as a Grain of Poppy Seed

Yes, we are small.
Who
under that noonblaze or
high midnight
wouldn't be?

But at sunset
or dawn
our shadows dwarf
the mountains they
never budge.

(Winter 1974)

Re-entry

unsickly wit to let the calves defend
my still calm body
but they nuzzled grass
and by their prowling kept the wolves away

into my back the flowers shoved
poppy nettle coltsfoot clover
and rosebay willow-herb
as though to re-assert
their briefly diverted mandate

the clouds had stalks, they
not drifting in the wind
swayed

the blue was almost black
a few pernicious stars
frayed the zenith
gamma fell with the light as hail in rain

somewhere in the distance
the voices of the recovery team
nit-picking shreds of my parachute

accelerating yet, a soul passed
its final puzzled words:
'But I thought Engels –'

the only heaven is annihilation

around me the module burned
its scattered fragments indecipherable

(1975)

Ham's Story

How did it take so long?
Imagine four
at such a task. The old man
crouched half the night over the sub-space radio,
cursing the static. Or stalked the streets
and market places, cursing the crowds
of gawkers, hawkers, merchants, whores
and mercenaries, who all ignored
the warnings he relayed from base
about the imminent axial tilt –
they had forgotten such a place
ever existed, or that our colony
was put here for a purpose.

It's no surprise that in later years
(between you and me)
he hit the wineskins hard
– but that's another story.

And all the while the rain,
the incessant storms,
the thunder-lizards cavorting on the plain
making it shudder like a dance-hall floor.

The other two up to their knees in shit
coping with the animals –
the arguments they had! Take this, leave that,
aquatic anyway, good to eat –

In the end
it was a natural selection.
We took the most evolved
and left the giant reptiles to their fate.

On top of that it was a part-time job –
yes! How else d'you think we paid
the rent, bought wood and power tools,
fed beasts and bairns
except by earning money?
And our wives in tears
often, from the poverty and ridicule.

That's why
building the Ark took me a hundred and twenty
    years.

(1976)

Stalin

How could anyone have swallowed
those tangles of barbed-wire?
Your unreadable works
Your unthinkable deeds
Your victims
screamed your praises
your beneficiaries
spit on your image

Yet some can still deny it all
and write 'Joe for King' on the shit-house wall.

Or say 'What about –

the slaves, the factory towns, the imperial wars
the liquidation of the crofters as a class?'

In the bodycount a mega-notch is carved.
How many peasants has the Free World starved?

'But this was different. This was deliberate.'

Is that your final condemnation?
Is that your ultimate
excuse?

No. You were not
the world-spirit in horse-
power. You marched
to the future backward
blind as the best of us, blinding
the rest
who endured the nightmare for the vision's sake

('there, beyond sorrow seas'
'when this fight is over'
'just around the corner')

and lived to see
at the end of the tunnel
darkness.

(Autumn 1974)

Caesarian

Two windows light the curtained room;
thro' one the summer air
infiltrates; thro' one we look
and see small portions of th' external world
in single vision multiplied, and we
who do not believe the lie, still
lie still and watch:
              'The chancellor today
held urgent talks on the current crisis
with the patrician and plebeian leaders
and owners of latifundia'
              (one of whom
the other day had an insolent slave
hacked up and fed to ornamental carp).

'In the metropolis there is growing concern
as yet another outpost of empire falls
to the barbarians'
              (who learned their national epic
from photocopies of the ancient manuscripts,
and quote its lines as slogans on the broken walls
while the defenders of civilization must move their
   lips
to read the words in their comic strips).

They who were with me in the gunships at Mylae
know there is a fate worse than death: decay.

As solar heat is focused by a lens
your after-image burns on my retinae.
How long have we got until the world ends?
You answer me in lunar months
unlucky fractions of years.

Conscripting this unborn draft-evader
to the defence of an order worse
than the worst disorder
is loyalty misplaced.
You fell on that sword
for an earlier Republic. On the telescreen
the veteran senator concludes his speech:
'Delenda est Carthago.' In the round
black mirror in the middle of your eye
only my troubled face reflects, as from
the remembered fishponds of a previous death.

(Summer 1975)

Birds and Bees and That

between rusty pylons
swifts dart like minnows
above the field of poppies and small
white flowers on giant stalks

in the wind the scent of the field shifts
like a fogbank of honey

what does the bee feel
as it clambers
around the flower?

your hair got in my mouth
your toes
tickled behind my knees which now
go loose as you grin at the sun

(1977)

Rosemergy

mind-matter:
           stone
               mint
                   gorse
                       heather
                           bracken
                               clover

cliff
sea from the grey horizon to the green
sea at the foot
long hollow metallic
crash
    one breaker
above the white noise of the white water

nicotine hit

I jump from rock to rock
on top of the stack
rock bays
fifty metres under either hand
and in the intervening air
the backs of the gulls and the black

                           birds

(1978)

Revolution

The sun's apparent rise
gets lower as the days
get shorter.

Edges are made sharp;
blood melts the snow
but briefly –

savages know
the point is to have the weapons
ready.

(1978)

Liberation

You drifted in
to my dark forests
and spread out
unnoticed.

Disquieted, I received
your triumphant communiqués
from one province after
another. Now
you flood the streets
of my capital.

What can I do
but welcome you
with cheering crowds?

(1979)

'Only a Flesh Wound'

To sugar-coated bullets from laughing guns
the paper tigers fell.
Unscathed the comic hero runs
through mortar, bayonet, shell.

Now rank on rank they rise up to accuse me –
Kraut and Tommy, Yank and Red.
By taking sides I've added them
to my private score or so of dead.

Not through our parents' chromosomes
is guilt transmitted, but their lives.
We cannot call our sin original.
It like the rest is plagiarized.

Our lives are built on the bones of slaves.
Those who rose with Spartacus
nailed up in thousands along the way
are who really died on the cross for us.

If so much more than power has grown
out of the barrel of a gun
why not the green tree, Ireland her own?
Imagined soldiers lay their charge, and run.

(1977)

Short March

The Cut –
a path that follows a watercourse
that follows a contour round the hills
to Loch Thom and the reservoirs
then joins a road that takes
you back behind those hills to where
you started –
this was our Yenan
the Sierra Maestra of our imaginations
where each weekend we took
our battered forces to recuperate, regroup
after six days of relentless reaction
at the hands of family, church and school;
we'd walk around it, talk, survey
from different vantages the triple town
whose indifference to the fevered futures
we foresaw for it was maybe for the best
and then stroll down
thumbs in our pockets, confident again
to its lighted streets to fight another day.

(1981)

The Word

First the Old Testament, then the New:
God, Son of God; Kings I, John II.
From Genesis to Revelation
it's a continuous cinema sensation.

The talking snake, the apple and the Flood,
the Exodus, the burning bush, the covenant of
    blood,
the locust plague, the holocaust, the chosen
    marching on,
the wisdom and the sexy song of great King
    Solomon.
The little carpenter gets nailed, then jumps up fit
    an' well –
turns out he's the Saviour who gets us outta hell!
The scenery is paramount, the imagery is rank.
From now to the apocalypse it's money in the
    bank.

Inspired by Disney and De Mille
the Book of Books was scripted for the screen.
(Goliath comes back in the final reel!
RSV, 2 Samuel 21, 19.)

(1984)

From Heraclitus

This world, which is the same for all
no god or man has made.
An ever-living fire it is
whose flames forever flare and fade.

(1984)

The Second Law

Through open door the factory's hiss;
sunlight patched on the wall across
from the cat on the dirty mat. It sniffs,
watches the flies – they dart and stop and
turn as if without inertia
easily evade the swatting claws
that severed scores of birds' and mammals' nerves.

Then the cat gives up, some coil unsprung.
The fridge begins to hum
started by thermostat, like the cat.
Cars pass, birds give voice
but who can say they sing, or engines roar.

Animals and machinery start and stop
their activity abruptly: homeostasis.
But when I turn
I feel inertia, facing choices.

(The way out is through the door.)

(1978)

View from a Point

I walk along the coast road
in the shadow of long streets
on a low hill. The Firth
is still as a lochan. Above
contrails crayon-in the early sky.

Across that water, nearby
behind green hills the mountains rise
like the books of the Old Testament,
older than life, older than light
from the visible firmament.
There, laws are stone. A single fault condemns
to fall and flood. There Jehovah prances.

Outworn by rain and air, rocks condescend
to take on raiment; earth and grass
becoming apple, sheep and man

who lifts the dust, made concrete, high again.
At the end of the breakwater I step into the sun.

(1986)

/*REMARKS

Alarm: off. Cursor: blink.
Clock: on. Conscience: clear.

We see nothing of the mind's working
except what comes on screen
and goes on keyboard. What's between
the two, behind the one –
the self that knows the self we know –
we don't know.

Memory: grains pebbles rocks
grass (see under BLADE). Pages,
word for word. Hair. Sparrows.
Falls. The ocean smell. Asphalt, chip by chip.
ENTER PASSWORD =>

SORRY, TRY AGAIN.

But every night this kid
steals in, hijacks the board,
calls up colour, sound,
hacks the access codes
for all the files
and uses them to play
sex fantasies, horror videos, home movies and
    adventure games

and (just as I reach to tap his shoulder)
logs
off. */

(1988)

Chain

Cape hunting dogs move in packs of twenty.
Hyenas' teeth are extra mild.

The wolf leaps from the silk cut –
it doesn't like the taste, but you
sure calm its nerves, give it a warm glow,
help it relax after a tense past.

The vultures describe cool thermals
waiting for that condor moment.

The worms are not impressed.
They roll their own.

(1988)

Fall 1991

The hammer rang in factory.
The sickle sang in field.
The kulak proved refractory.
The hammer made the sickle yield.

Nature in claw and tooth is red
    – not Red enough for us, it seems.
Despite the millions of accusing dead
all animals are equal in our dreams.

Chew the worm and spit away the apple.
Fat of the heartland, sucrose fed.
The rich man passes through the needle.
The rest of us just get it in the head.

(1992)

Succession

In Uig the ruined walls, like giants' bones
lie under turf. You see between the hills
old roads that lead you nowhere now, that once
were black with cattle, loud with men.

Through tens of miles of intersecting glens
the brochs command a view, and so display
an earlier battle. Those who won were left
the standing stones, the seed, the memories
of people before the people they
left dead.

The roads wind back through Dane and Celt and
    Pict
and back: Neanderthal, Cro-Magnon Man,
the beings we might have been walk deserted
    tracks
as dwarf and giant. Buried in our bones
in convoluted glens within our heads
in trackless chromosomes a swifter race
prepares the day when we
step over stones
on grass-green motorways are seen behind
the eyes another people call their own.

(1993)

Goddess on Our Side

Her nerves are cables, roads her veins;
we are her cells, our cities flexed
knots of muscle, wars her pains,
voyaging probes her fingertips.

Her breath is whisper, clamour, text.
Her dreams are shining silver ships.

Her thoughts are aeroplanes.

(1993)

The Morlock's Arms

The wasps are big this year, the meteors
green in the summer night. Our land
ironclads are far away, our flying-machines
visit atrocity on innocence. We do not care.
This is the World State. We're a planet now.

Our empire was the sun,
famine or fusillade its worst extreme,
its best a world that turned
on a war we fought, in the air.

And we're still here, in the light,
we Morlocks, we whose corpses
rotted conveniently in the cosy catastrophe,
we feckless, toothless proles, feral cattle
for whom entropy was never cool.

No Empire now, nor New Jerusalem,
no Modern Utopia. Only the streets
of Earth and England

and a sense of something about to happen.
Because we never went away
we will think of something
in our own time, gentlemen. Please.

(2000)

After Burns: 11 September 2002

An empty threat can empty skies:
no contrail-crayon crosses
that pale blue dome. But come on, guys!
We can do better. Losses

are not made less but multiplied
and fear's increased by flinches.
We but dishonour those who died
in dying ourselves by inches.

When in the daylight laws are made
in halls that all may enter,
there's light at night, a world of trade,
a world where Man's the centre.

There is no God, and we must get
our comfort where we find it:
in the rising yell of a laden jet
and a bright contrail behind it.

(2002)

One for the Carpenter

Happy birthday to you,
Josh Davidson! Who-
ever you were, you
could never be nailed,
planed, sanded, dove-tailed
to cross or crib.
Joiner, leader, agitator, king;
teller and told in contrary
stories; healer with a sword –
here's a word in your ear:
I wish you Merry Christmas
and a Happy New Year.

Two thousand and three
candles and counting:
we can stop holding our breath:

you're not coming back.
But you're still here, walking
in writing on water,
in vexed texts talking
at cross purposes.

Against the rough
places, still not smooth,
the high places, still not low
still Mary's hand lights a candle: blow.

(2003)

Scots Poet, Not

I cannae write in Scots. It's no my tongue
nor Gaelic neither. That option was foreclosed.
My parents spake the Beurla in the hame
tae break that chain while I wis young.

Alienation was a consequence
and felt injustice an early rage.
The sex, the sect, the colour of the skin
in the licht of sin ground-in irrelevance.

Famine and eviction were an unsettled score.
Eat up your food or you'll lick where it lay.
Martyr and murderer, rebel and traitor
were one in the Covenant, so ho whiggamore!

Tae see oorsels as wicked frae the start
is greater gift than by the maist supposed.
What was done to us, and what we did
is worse by far than aught we proposed.

Thanks be to Knox and Calvin, we were rid
of any hesitation of the heart.
MacDiarmid and Maclean spake weel of Lenin.
Them I cannae blame. It was a start.

It stops wi me, like sae muckle else:
the Gaelic and the Lallans and the nane tae help,
the wicked frae the start tae see oorsels,
the Shorter Catechism and the skelp.

(2005)

Beurla (pronounced approximately *bare*-la): the English
    language
whiggamore: Covenanter of 1648, reputedly from their cry
    while spurring their horses towards Edinburgh; hence also
    Whig.
maist: most, majority
muckle: much
Lallans: Lowland Scots dialect
skelp: slap

A Fertile Sea

for Iain Banks
who walked by sight

I. Waste Disposal

It is interesting to contemplate a tangled bank
clothed with many plants of many kinds
birds singing in the bushes
insects flitting about
and to reflect
that six separate safety checks
were deliberately overridden
we may look with some confidence
to a secure future of great length.

We sat, you and I, and talked to her half the night
drinking export and whisky and wine
The smokes came like dogs, in packs, and were
    gone
(but her hair was still there, curling around her
    face)
She listened amused, unbelieving not what we said
but that we said it. Orbital factories, asteroid
    mining,
Apollo Soyuz, shuttles weaving
emptiness into webs of electric speech

a Soviet America: take it either way, or both
– freedom of choice, *da*? 'You're crazy, guys.'

The engineer, one of Zhukov's men,
was there when they took the camp.
He told me what they found:
conveyor belts
powered by treadmills, rocket engines
dragged along on sleds.
Hurrying to the office, Herr von Braun
didn't see the hanged men every day.

We kissed her goodbye with the meter ticking

Stop the nuclear train
It isn't rain it's fallout
Nuclear waste fades your genes
   clear was   our gen

from so simple a beginning, endless forms
have been endowed by their creator with certain
inalienable rights, among them
Lakenheath, Tripoli, Benghazi
what lies under the rubble, baby?
OK THAT'S ENOUGH CUT
ten seconds of tendril fingers clutching
air shows lack of balance, lady.

'I'm too old to die,' she grinned
as she powdered white her face (her hair
would do as it was) and took her place
carefully selecting a dry spot on the platform
to lie down on, covered with a bin-sack

while I zipped into a rad-suit. A lovely girl
Friend of the Earth smiled and gave me a bunch
of leaflets. I waited nervously
as the dark gathered. The crowds came in boxes of
    light
spilling out on the platform, stepping carefully
over the old comrades, the dead on leave
while we sinister hooded figures
stepped up and asked for their signatures.

II. Arcadia Games

She swung in her Highbury hammock
and brushed her metre-long red flag
of hair as if it was an enemy. This is a rich room
that makes no concessions
to interior decorators. Polish embroideries,
Russian scarves, posters from two decades,
three continents. African masks, a low gas-fire,
Lenin on the hearth, Marx
and Madhur Jaffrey on the shelves.

'We stayed nine years in Prague.
The first three
were great, peace and socialism, yeah!
The next three we began to see some problems
and he'd come home in a sweat as if
drenched with rain. It isn't that there's queues,
just shortages.' She laughs. 'But then, for the last
    three
we learned also what there's plenty of,
and, let me tell you, it's damn scarce here.'

Yes, but will you take your card for another year?
We went down to the pub to talk about it.
She sank pints and smashed me
at Asteroids, Pac-Man and Missile Command.

Turn off the aiming computer. Look.
Here
behind the irony curtain
where everything has happened
and nothing has changed.

Free to choose. Labour isn't working.
Trust the Force. We are not listening,
merely recording. Remain in your seats.
The stars are your destiny, not your destination.
The post-modern Prince has criticized
the architecture of the Finland Station.
Peace through mutual . . . let us here pause
and consider the various (if ultimately
harmonious, convergent, reinforcing)
conclusions that succeeding
idealists whose sincerity we do not for one
   moment
impugn, would provide
and (returning the debate to a serious level)
proceed to . . . assured destruction.

From Plato to Nato, from Albert Speer to
Albert Square, we have ways of keeping you quiet.
Have you a bad memory? Let us help you forget.
Don't die of ignorance. Why be alone?
Have your Tarot read over the phone!
(Interlude: white noise.)

We remind you to turn off your set.

III. Writing in Water

Firth, neither sea nor river,
oh my Clyde you carry such a weight.
The coracles are gone, the fishing-smacks, the
    merchant-
ships, the rigs. Only the yachts and canoes,
the tankers and the base remain;
the heavy water and the hot metal.
I feel that throw-weight on my back
under the suface, of Cumbrae.
Refracted by water, air and glass
the sunlight radiates, its centre everywhere
my eyes can rest, its rim beyond
where I can see. The snorkel stops
my breath to save me –
to gasp under water, and not to drown!
Will you see any clearer from a glass shore?

I shrug on futures like old clothes,
the uniforms of long-disbanded corps.
Uninstructed, we defended
our dishonoured republics. Our eyes stung
to tear-gas in Baltic ports; we measured
progress in yards. Naked, you outstrip me;
scratch the surface: under the veneer
of barbarism I'm a decadent sophisticate.
You come with open eyes, I turn aside
because behind those eyes a brain

goes on working while my mind leaves
like a flock of birds from a tree.

I saw you strong and free, like the future.
You saw
what Althusser saw: the structures
replicate across time like molecules in a cheap
    graphic.
You heard
the silences, like Luria walking his wards
of shattered veterans piecing worlds together.
You felt
the strain of Maclean's grasp on the dock
saying, 'I have squared my conduct with my
    intellect,'
or Gramsci and Galileo: '*E pur si muove.*'
So for your weakness I have no aid, though from
    your strength
I've taken more than you'll ever know,
or I can tell. As dawn displays
the flag above the factory
the world is back where it always was.

The day came when the soldiers went away.
The discotheque became a crèche.
Mrs Campbell had a lovely daughter,
lost a son on San Carlos water.
Her daddy owned an aluminium smelter
a Swiss account and a fallout shelter.

We fall back
to the harder task
of building love
vaster than Internationals and more slow
and with an engineer's exactitude
an adequate instrument, ourselves.

IV. Challenger

Remember Komarov
Remember Grissom, White, Chaffee
Remember Dobrovolsky, Volkov, Patsayev
Remember Resnick, Scobee, Smith, McNair,
McAuliffe, Jarvis, Onizuka
when you walk the sea beds of the moon
when you hang-glide
the valley of the Mariners
when you turn
slow cartwheels in the solar meadows
remember Nordhausen

V. What the Lightning Showed

As if the Lewisian gneiss was split
straight down, then hauled a quarter mile apart
– some thought it was, at the Passion
when the rocks rent.
It was cut by the quiet burn
that still shifts pebbles along its floor.
It held the sunlit air like an echoing shout
the day I climbed one side and, looking down
thought I was afraid of the height, then thought
I was afraid of the light and the silence
and then was unafraid of the light and the silence
and then was unafraid. In other glens,
on other cliffs the sense became familiar,
the panic returning like a friend
who startles then reveals
who it was, all the time.

Like white sticks the headlamp beams
probed the fog as we inched towards the border.
Crossing under watchful muzzles, we found
ourselves in another order: history frozen
into geography – a mountain-building episode
that segregates varieties into species
and thence to genus, family, order, class, division,
    kingdom.
Barbed wire mutates from barricades, heresiarchs
emblazon graffiti into heraldry.
The haunted continent reflects

and makes its own hair stand on end.
Expecting tanks and sullen people
I found monuments and snug-wrapped children.
We made our dead-letter drops and fled.

The helicopters came in low, towards Halabja.
Blind Cretaceous tanks
struggled in mud. The dead lay
unmarked, the children
like dolls that children had not put away.

One man had put his body between his child
and the expected (allowed for, discounted) blast
but could not stop the breath that stopped the
    breath.

Don't talk to me, you slaughtering saints –
I know these people, possessed
of every human attribute but one: the State;
and for this lack you compensate, provide
the solicitude of more than one, supplied
in an impressive range of delivery systems
from I G Farben to Ilyushin.

Fom space you can see no borders;
only the Iran–Iraq border, drawn in fire.
What look like shadows are only corpses.
The third man circled overhead.
On that waterless rock I remember joy
– to fall, and rise unhurt, like children
where dust and dirt
for once are not the same as earth.
You can blot it out with your thumb.

We have a problem here.
V2, SDI.

Obviously a major malfunction.
Ulan-Bator, do you read?
Da: what is to be done?

Sparks from a fierce far forge, the particles
penetrate helmet, hair and bone
and passing through the brain leave
a flash behind the eyes.
As much as anyone can see, I've seen
a greater death than mine will be,
or birth. There is still no agreement.

Data: what are we given?
A manipulated nucleus of time
where our fortunes and our futures recombine.
We are not born to trouble, we can make
the sparks fly downward.
We can send the cities skyward, stone by stone
and call them new: New Jerusalem,
New Cairo, New Berlin, New London,
New Moscow, New New York.

Under white hoods they crossed the ice
already melting. The gulf took some, the sleeting
    particles
took others who fought to contain
a reaction's red glare.
Those who knew themselves
already dead stood by the living.

For so much less than this
for so much less
for so much

new lands no prophet promised
are there for you
oh turn your back
you who could fall for borders
for inches of mud, for acres of rock
for tons of sand
oh turn your back
on controlling hands, on lands and orders
rank and waste
rack and ruin

Take you the sky, and give them their deserts:
no peace, no shelter, no surrender.

Notes on 'A Fertile Sea'

The poem is in more senses than one a *reaction* to T. S. Eliot's 'The Waste Land'. The allusions are scientific and political, the perspective is secular and humanist, the poem is comparatively short, and the notes are explanatory. (Actually, they were even more tedious, needless and pretentious than Eliot's, and have been dropped.)

I wrote this poem in the late 1980s. I've sometimes tried to revise it since, but it's so much a product of its time that revising it would have lost its directness. The allusions to (and suggested connections between) the Chernobyl nuclear disaster, the US air raid on Libya, the Iran–Iraq War, the decline and internal disintegration of the communist parties, the failed renewal of the socialist bloc, the experiences of astronauts and cosmonauts in lunar and orbital expeditions, the military origins of the space programme, and the suppression of the Kronstadt uprising are too obvious to need elucidation.

Index of First Lines

Iain Banks

Index of First Lines

Ken MacLeod